Celebrate Wha?
Ten Black British Poets from the Midlands
edited by Eric Doumerc and Roy McFarlane

Published 2011by
Smokestack Books
PO Box 408, Middlesbrough TS5 6WA
e-mail : info@smokestack-books.co.uk
www.smokestack-books.co.uk

Celebrate Wha?
Ten Black British Poets from the Midlands
Cover image: *Fragments 3* by Vanley Burke

Printed by
EPW Print & Design Ltd

ISBN 978-0-9568144-0-1
Smokestack Books gratefully
acknowledges the support of
Arts Council England

LOTTERY FUNDED

Smokestack Books is
represented by Inpress Ltd
www.inpressbooks.co.uk

'The poet is a mediator between the ruler and the ruled, as an inciter, a moulder of opinions, a social critique. He is not only concerned to chronicle the deeds of and qualities of the ancestors of his contemporaries. He also responds poetically to the social and political circumstances confronting him at the time of their performance'.
Jeff Opland, 'The Isolation of the Xhosa Poet',
Xhosa Poets and Poetry

'A bird doesn't sing because it has an answer, it sings because it has a song'.
Maya Angelou

5/13

DATE DUE FOR RETURN

Cc

Renewals
www.liverpool.gov.uk/libraries
0151 233 3000

Contents

Foreword

Celebrate Wha?, is an anthology that presents and celebrate poetry written by ten poets in and around the Birmingham area. The title suggests irreverence, a mocking of these times. What is there to celebrate? Moqapi Selassie is succinct and direct in his response to the 2007 celebrations that were focused mostly on the achievements of William Wilberforce. He gives an alternative celebration, names that reflect an African history, rich and diverse bringing us to the present day.

I believe the poems in this anthology explore aspects of life, environment, spirituality, music and families. A carnival of poetry that portrays the life and culture of people living in Birmingham as well as looking at issues that continue to affect our community, locally and globally; *celebrate wha?* when racism, inequalities, injustice, gun crime and economic upheavals continue to afflict our neighbourhoods.

This collection is about who we are as poets from the African diaspora. I use the term African diaspora to link all the poets but it is important to recognise the different journeys within this anthology. Many of the poets are first and second generation children of the Caribbean migration to England in the late 1950s and 1960s, other poets were born in the Caribbean and are residing over here and there are those whose parents are inclusive of British and Asian heritage. And with so many different identities and journeys, how does this manifest itself amongst different generations of poets living and working in Birmingham and surrounding areas?

The poetry within these pages is often intense and personal; internal and introspective; challenging with a social narrative; and at times a simple reflection of the world around us. They have been hewn out of life experience, forged in the crucibles of live audiences. There is a desire for them to be owned by the public, at times aimed at a certain constituency that understands the injustice, the struggle and the immediacy for change.

They are living, breathing poems, declaring the colour of skin, the beauty of language, or the essence of heritage. Read them aloud and you feel the energy in each syllable, words full of life, to be spoken, to be released outside the confines of verse and page. *Celebrate Wha?* is an inciter, a social critique responding to issues at the time of his/her performance.

The poets have performed in cafes, clubs, pubs, theatre, libraries, at book festivals, cultural events, conferences and slam/performance poetry events. Poets who have gone on to being regulars on radio and TV. They have shared and worked together on the stage, formed groups and collectives such as The Conscious Poets Society of the 1990s and more recently the New October Poets of the noughties.

There is also the influence of Roi Kwabena who has touched, encouraged and developed many of the poets in the collective. Roi Kwabena and Eric Doumerc successfully published *Five Birmingham Poets* under Raka Books in 2006. Roi's desire to go further and develop another book called, *10 Birmingham Poets* was unfortunately never achieved due to his untimely death in 2008.

Martin Glynn, who appeared in *Five Birmingham Poets*, is the Godfather of poetry in the Birmingham area. He came into prominence back in the 1980s, closely followed by Moqapi Selassie, Sue Brown, and Chester Morrison all four who have had international acclaim.

The next group of poets, Marcia Calame, Kokumo, Dreadlockalien, Michelle Hubbard, and Roy McFarlane came into prominence at the turn of the Millennium and have established regional, national and international status.

And finally Evoke gives us a flavour of the next generation whose poetry is youthful, but mature, relevant to these times, whose identity is sure-footed, allowing them to explore so many avenues through their poetry.

These poets don't 'do poetry' because they have an answer. These poets do poetry because they have it flowing through their pens, emanating from their voices, gesticulating from their performances. Share with us this celebration of poetry.

Roy McFarlane
Birmingham

Introduction

After the Second World War many immigrants from the West Indies came to Britain in search of better living and working conditions, better-paid jobs. These people came for different reasons and usually distinctions are made between 'push' and 'pull' factors. The push factors included the unbearable living conditions in certain colonies. The pull factors included cultural reasons: many immigrants had been made to feel British by the colonial education system based on the study of the classics of English literature.

Economic reasons were important too. Britain had been bombed during the war and certain areas of London (the East End) as well as the city of Coventry had been completely flattened out during the Battle of Britain. England's road system had been seriously damaged too. So after the Second World War the main task facing Clement Attlee's Labour government was to rebuild the country. Numerous jobs were available in the building industry. There was also a labour shortage in the public transport sector and in the expanding NHS. Consequently the government launched a policy of encouragement to immigration from the Commonwealth and the first immigrants came from the West Indies (Jamaica, Barbados, Trinidad, Guyana).

In 1948, 492 Jamaicans disembarked from the SS Empire Windrush at Tilbury. There were already several thousand non-white Britons, mainly in ports like Liverpool, Bristol and Cardiff. At first most immigrants came from the West Indies, but during the 1960s and 1970s a large number came from India, Pakistan and Bangladesh. The early immigrants soon became the target of discrimination in housing, employment and at school and, in 1958, violent race riots erupted in Notting Hill Gate (in West London): black immigrants were attacked by white youths and Britain suddenly realised that it had a racial problem. In 1958 Nottingham was rocked by race riots too.

In the 1960s more and more immigrants came to Britain; in the first ten months of 1961, 113,000 people arrived in Britain from India, Pakistan and the Caribbean. Violent reactions against immigrants became more and more common (the National Front appeared) and the government soon introduced the first anti-immigration measures. The various Labour and Conservative governments passed several laws to restrict the flow of immigrants (the Commonwealth Immigration Acts) and then to protect immigrants from discrimination (the 1965,1968 and 1976 Race Relations Acts). The early Caribbean immigrants went to London, but also to the Midlands, which became the second area of black settlement in England. Black Caribbean people settled down in Liverpool, Leeds, Bristol and Bradford too. Many men had to take low-paid jobs (building, bus-driving). Many women worked as nurses in the NHS or as cleaners.

The West Midlands conurbation (Birmingham, Coventry, Solihull, Dudley, Willenhall, Wednesbury, Wolverhampton) became a home from home for the early migrants and then simply home for the Black British generation born in Britain of West Indian parentage. The East Midlands, with Nottingham and Leicester, also have their own West Indian communities.

It is well-known that the Black Caribbean presence in the Midlands gave birth to a new musical tradition, British reggae, with bands like Steel Pulse and UB40, and contributed to the Two Tone ska revival in the late 1970s/early 1980s with bands like The Beat, The Specials (from Coventry) and the Selecter. The cross-pollination of punk, rockabilly and reggae produced interesting hybrid forms and the region is now on the map as a great mecca for reggae and ska lovers.

Nevertheless, in spite of the region's musical preeminence, the poetic contribution of West Midlands black poetry has always been either ignored or overlooked.

Black British poetry developed in Britain thanks to the work done by independent publishing houses like New Beacon

Books founded in 1966 by the Guyanese poet John LaRose, and Bogle L'Ouverture Publications started in 1969 by Eric and Jessica Huntley. The *Race Today* Collective was also important and brought out Linton Kwesi Johnson's first collection in 1974 (*Voices of the Living and the Dead*). In the 1970s Black British poetry was dominated by Linton Kwesi Johnson who published two more collections of poetry (*Dread Beat an' Blood* in 1975, and *Inglan is a Bitch* in 1980). In 1976 an important anthology of Black British poetry was put together by the poet James Berry, *Bluefoot Traveller: Poetry by Westindians in Britain*. This anthology included poems by Linton Kwesi Johnson, James Berry and Jimi Rand among others and introduced many readers to the delight of the Caribbean oral tradition.

In 1982 New Beacon Books, Bogle L'Ouverture Publications and the *Race Today* Collective pooled their resources to organise the first International Book Fair of Radical Black and Third World Books in Islington. This major event gathered poets like John Agard, Valerie Bloom, James Berry, Linton Kwesi Johnson, Edward Kamau Brathwaite and the late Mikey Smith, and was another important milestone in the greater visibility of Caribbean poetry in Britain.

In 1984 James Berry edited a new anthology entitled *News for Babylon* which was published by Chatto and Windus. This collection featured poems by John Agard, Valerie Bloom, Levi Tafari, and Benjamin Zephaniah and these poets revitalised Black British poetry in the 1980s. In 1985 the poet Desmond Johnson founded Akira Press which brought out collections by Marsha Prescod, Desmond Johnson, J.D. Douglas, and a young poet from the Midlands named Martin Glynn (*De Ratchet a Talk*).

Following the publication of his second collection, *The Dread Affair*, in 1985, Benjamin Zephaniah became a major figure on the performance poetry scene and most of his books were published by Bloodaxe Books. John Agard and Grace Nichols also contributed immensely to the popularisation of Caribbean/Black British poetry thanks to the work they did in schools and of course through their numerous publications.

More recently, an important anthology of Black British writing was edited in 1998 by the poet Lemn Sissay. *The Fire People* (Payback Press, 1998) was an innovative anthology which gathered poems by Patience Agbabi, Jackie Kay, Vanessa Richards, Roger Robinson and Tricky among others and introduced many readers to new talented writers.

2002 saw the publication of *Moving Voices – Black Performance Poetry* (Hansib, 2002), a collection edited by Asher and Martin Hoyles. The book's general introduction set the poems in their proper cultural and historical context. Due emphasis was laid on the importance of the African, African-American and Afro-Caribbean oral traditions which have contributed to shaping and nurturing today's dynamic Black British poetry. The various components of 'orature' like proverbs, folk tales, riddles, songs, jazz and blues are all related to the poetic creative process and this is clearly emphasized by the authors.

Lastly, and most importantly, the book included a CD with recordings of the poems anthologised. The importance of this CD cannot be overemphasized as oral poetry is often said to require oral verbalization to achieve its full effect. The accompanying CD gave the reader the opportunity to hear what performance poets like Patience Agbabi or Benjamin Zephaniah sound like in a live setting and consequently to appreciate the power of oral poetry. More recently, in 2010, Peepal Tree Press brought out an anthology of Black British poetry entitled *Red: Contemporary Black British Poetry*, edited by Kwame Dawes and Kadija Sesay and including poems by John Agard, Grace Nichols and Linton Kwesi Johnson among others. In September 2010 Bloodaxe Books published *Ten New Poets Spread the Word*, an anthology of poems by Black and Asian poets edited by Bernadine Evaristo and Daljit Nagra. This anthology includes poems by Malika Booker and Roger Robinson.

The poets whose work appears in this anthology are all of West Indian parentage and, with the exception of Kokumo, were all born in Britain. They belong to the Black British generation and thus have a double perspective on life, a West Indian/Jamaican take on things, and a more British one. For them, culture always means something more than British culture or Jamaican culture: it is always a process, it is always in flux.

The book is divided into four sections in order to reflect the diversity of approaches that can be found today in Black British poetry in the West and East Midlands. The first section is devoted to the dub poetry tradition which is here represented by Moqapi Selassie and Kokumo (Gerald Dixon). The words 'dub poetry' refer to a brand of oral poetry which developed in Jamaica and in England in the 1970s thanks to the work done by poets like Mutabaruka, Orlando Wong (Oku Onuora) and Linton Kwesi Johnson. In an interview granted to the critic Mervyn Morris in 1979 Oku Onuora defined a dub poem as 'a poem that has a built-in reggae rhythm - hence when the poem is read without any reggae rhythm (so to speak) backing, one can distinctly hear the reggae rhythm coming out of the poem'.

In Jamaica, Oku Onuora published his first collection of poetry, *Echo*, while he was serving a prison sentence for armed robbery. The authorities allowed him out of prison to perform his poetry. In 1981 he released two records, *Reflection in Red* and *Wat a Situashan*, on which he performed his poems to the accompaniment of reggae music.

Similar experiments with sound and music had been carried out in England by the Black British poet Linton Kwesi Johnson who was born in Jamaica in 1952 and arrived in England in 1961. LKJ also recorded a number of reggae albums with Island Records and then Virgin, and these recordings made him very popular with a young, multicultural audience which was probably more interested in reggae than in poetry.

In his poems Johnson dealt with the problems faced by the West Indian and Black British community in Britain and he quickly became the voice of Black Britain. His poems relied heavily on reggae rhythms and frequently featured binary structures and alliteration.

The poems by Moqapi Selassie and Kokumo in this anthology clearly belong to the dub poetry tradition in which the poet is primarily seen as a bard, as a troubadour whose task consists in raising people's consciousness. The poet's role in such a tradition recalls that of the DJ in Jamaican popular music and the 1970s DJs I-Roy, Big Youth and Prince Far-I may have served as inspiration for many young dub poets in the 1970s and 1980s. Moqapi Selassie himself used to work with a sound system in the 1980s. Moqapi's 'Rigmarole Game' addresses the important issues of international aid and Third World economic dependency. 'Celebrate Wha?' deals with the issue of the commemoration of the abolition of the British slave trade in 1807 (slavery of course was not abolished in Britain until 1833). The bicentenary in 2007 was commemorated in various ways, in museums, schools, on television, on the radio, and in many newspaper columns. The official version of that commemoration tended to lay the emphasis on the contribution made by famous abolitionist leaders like William Wilberforce, Thomas Fowell Buxton and Granville Sharp, and on the role of parliamentary channels in the fight against slavery. It is quite obvious that without the political influence of the abolitionist movement, slavery would not have been abolished so early (France abolished slavery in 1848). Nevertheless Moqapi Selassie gives us another version of the story, a version which has already been discussed by historians like Richard Hart and James Walvin. That version emphasises the importance of slave rebellions in the Caribbean, and the contribution made by black leaders like Tacky, Nanny of the Maroons, and Sam Sharpe. The latter led the 'Emancipation Rebellion' or 'Baptist War' in 1831-32, which is said to have precipitated the abolition of slavery in 1833.

Kokumo's 'Check Out Mista Govament Man' attacks injustice at all levels, but mainly institutional and his 'In Too Deep' tackles the issue of drug addiction in an urban context. This poem is in standard English, and shows that dub poetry need not necessarily be in dialect or Creole to make its point forcefully.

The second section, entitled 'Storytelling and Voice', presents the work of two women poets: Sue Brown, from Birmingham, and Michelle Hubbard, aka The Mother, from Nottingham. With these two poets, the emphasis moves from protest to a quieter voice, a voice which comments on life and its ups-and-downs, love, but also ancestral culture. The poems featured in this section capture experiences which are intrinsically Black British, and the meeting of Jamaican culture with British or English culture is a recurrent theme. Thus in Michelle Hubbard's poems Anansi the Spider gets reincarnated in Robin Hood Country and W.H. Auden meets modern urban street talk. Humour is also present in these pieces. Check out Sue Brown's 'Pain'.

The third section is made up of poems written by Marcia Calame, Martin Glynn and Roy McFarlane. These poems are proof that Black British poetry can also be about introspection and the inner life, as is shown by Marcia Calame's 'Spring Clean'. The personal journey is also a major theme in Martin Glynn's autobiographical 'To Whom It May Concern', a poem which charts the persona's development through the various stages of life. Martin's 'Where It's At' looks at issues like masculinity and the humanity that we all share.

Roy McFarlane's quiet pieces reflect both an awareness of roots and a desire to engage with life in Britain. Humour is never far from the surface. Read 'It's Snowing Outside'. Identity is an important concern both in Marcia's poems ('Going Dutch', 'Speak English') and in Roy's pieces ('A Black Man in Wolverhampton'), but the power of words, and of poetry, is equally important (see Roy's 'Leaving Me in Throes of Ecstasy').

The fourth section is devoted to the 'new' forms of performance poetry which have been developing in Britain for a number of years now: slam and grime. Slam first developed in the USA, in Chicago more precisely, and then spread to various countries. It is a competitive type of oral poetry and at slam events the audience judges the poets' performances and awards them points. In Birmingham the foremost exponent of slam is Dreadlockalien (Richard Grant), a poet from Rugby who won the National Slam Championship in 2003 and has not looked back since. Richard is also a workshop facilitator and with his Colour Free Visions Team takes poetry to schools as part of the government's current literacy programme. His poems are oral pieces which use repetition and dialect a lot, and which often deal with the theme of his double heritage ('Anglo-Indo-Caribbean'). The influence of Benjamin Zephaniah's poetry is clearly visible in his approach. Richard tackles the issue of political correctness and irony is never far from the surface in his poetry. Evoke defines himself as a spoken-word artist and his popularity has been growing over the years. He works in a style known as hip hop/rap or grime, which is associated with East London, but his poems in this anthology are in standard English and deal with very personal and universal themes, proof that Black British performance poetry is moving forward and reaching out.

Language and identity are obviously very important for all these poets, and some of them use dialect/Creole or a Creole-inflected English in their poems. Moqapi Selassie, Kokumo, and Dreadlockalien, the poets situated at the oral end of the language continuum, tend to use Creole more. When faced with poems in Creole or in Creole-inflected English, the anthologist can either standardise the spelling, using Cassidy and Le Page's guidelines, or keep the spelling system used by the poets, however idiosyncratic and confusing it may be for the hapless readers. This anthologist decided to retain the original spelling system for two reasons. Firstly, it seems to me that the system used by the poets in the present anthology is a reasonable guide to pronunciation and is not too confusing, provided these poems are read out loud. So please, sound them out! Secondly, keeping the original spelling allows us to relish each poet's individual approach and idiosyncrasy. Nevertheless, for the sake of clarity, I decided to add punctuation marks, or modify punctuation, where it was felt that the absence of punctuation made the poems difficult to understand.

This anthology owes a great debt of gratitude to many people who have worked hard over the years to nurture and develop poetry in the Midlands. Simon Fletcher has been hosting City Voices events in Wolverhampton for many years, while Colour Free Visions Team, a collective of poets from different backgrounds, have been taking poetry into schools. The poet and troubadour Dave Reeves edited the Arts Council-funded magazine *Raw Edge* between 1995 and 2008 and thus contributed to keeping poetry alive in the Midlands by publishing work by new poets, and by providing a wealth of information about events and festivals. *Raw Edge* ceased publication in 2008 but Dave now runs *Radio Wildfire* an internet community radio which broadcasts once a month and delivers a steady diet of spoken word, storytelling, music, and poetry. West Midlands poets regularly appear on the show. More information about Radio Wildfire can be gleaned at www.radiowildfire.com. The late Roi Kwabena, originally from Trinidad, lived in Birmingham for many years and was a tireless promoter of other people's work, conducting countless workshops and giving talks at various events. His own imprint, Raka Books, brought out many valuable poetic works. Roi was Birmingham Poet Laureate in 2001-2002 and did his best to promote Birmingham as a potential City of Culture.

Eric Doumerc
University of Toulouse-Le Mirail, Toulouse, France

Dub

Moqapi Selassie

Moqapi Selassie has been performing in the West Midlands for many years, including appearances at the Ledbury festival, the Round Festival in Wimborne, the Birmingham Readers and Writers Festival, the Cave, the Midlands Arts Centre and the Drum. In July 2002 he opened for Burning Spear at the Birmingham Academy.

A few years ago he was featured in a documentary by the French/German TV channel Arte on the Birmingham riots in Handsworth. He recently staged a one-man show entitled *Blackheart Man*, charting the experience of growing up as a black person in England in the 1970s. Some of his poems can be found in *Black Men and Black women in Love* (Osiris Publications, 1997) and in *Five Birmingham Poets* (Raka Books, 2006).

Rigmarole Game

Peepul are dyin as I speek,
dyin fa lack a food fi eat.
An while food mountinz are rottin,
politishanz ah give big speech.

Teechaz teech,
preechaz preech.
I will chant an rant
an beseech:
'ow komz nuttins appenin
I beg unu put sum food
inna di starvinz reech!'

Yuh nuh tiyad
fi si di same pikcha
flik up pan yuh TV screen,
starvin perents an chiljren
inna Afrika.
Iz wa appm? Demmah nuh hewman been?
Demmah wait fi peepul dead fuss
before dem deside fi intaveen
den demmah taak bout hewmaniteariyan aid
wen dem fly dem planes
wid food an medsn een.
Iz ow dem fine dem tings suh kwikly
mirakewlusly tons ov food appear.
Gweh yah man!!
Nuh mek dem fool yuh:
di mountinz ov food woz always dere
iz jus dat demmah wait
fi certn mount a peepul dead arf
before di uddah res a peepul dem get dem share.
Den demmah kom in di name of relijan,
pretendin dat dem reely kyere
Chu!!!

Peepul are dyin as I speek.
A bom jus went arf in di street,
an whilse di arms trayde is flourishin,
politishanz a give big speech.

Politishanz ah taak long time bout peace
inna afrika, yewrup, di miggle eese,
di karribeyond an inna di far eese.
But instead a di war an violence decrease,
it luk like it gaan pon di increase
bad bwoy, soljah an poleese
ah kill arf dem wan anudda outta street.
A yoot wi kill a nex yoot fi di leese,
den dem lok im inna jail wid nu early release
wake up from yuh slumbah an yuh sleep
coz I will chant an rant an beseech:
'ow kom nuttingz changing
I beg unu ah time di war an violence cease!'

Peepul are dyin as I speek.
Aids dets inna Afrika
reech a new peek,
an whilst di
farmahsewtikal kompanees are rejoysin
di Afrikan race is bekumin absahleet.

Kkyaan afford Afrika tuh get defeet.
Demmah tek Afrika's resources coz
Afrika is weak.
Dem deh pon a mishan an it almous kompleet.
I a guh tell yuh ow I see't,
Coz I nuh kom yah fi kin teet.
Teet an tung it a guh meet
An Jah Jah no it nah guh sweet.
Genaside a gwaan an yuh jus kyaan see't.
Evvry fifteen sekanz tru aids
A Afrikan life cease
Afrikan life expektansy
Is on di decrease.
Chile mortality is on di increase.

yuh tink seh a it dat
dat a jus di leese
korrup diktaytahz, politishanz,
soljahz an poleese
bizniz men, lawyahz an big chiefs
ah du di dutty wuk
fi kolowneeyal teefs,
whiles dem peepul nah nuh food fi eat
demmah drink shampayn an a nyam
dem bluddy bluddy meat,
but I will chant an rant an beseech:
'ow komz nuttinz appenin,
iz time dis RIGMAROLE GAME cease'.

Celebrate Wha?

*for the bicentenary of the abolition of the British slave trade in
1807 (after which it was illegal to trade in slaves, although
perfectly legal to own them)*

Celebrate wha
di abolishan
ov slayvree
afta mi nu mad
afta mi nu krayzee.
Celebrate wha
di abolishan
ov slayvree.
As far as I kyan see
Afrikanz still nu free

I will not be defined
by your
babilownian terms
or be infected by your laboratory-designed germs.
I free I mind
rom your intellectual captivity,
your psychological
chicanery,
your political skulduggery.
I will not be bound
by your negative word sound.

I am NO SLAVE.
I have been ENSLAVED.
I was a PRISONER OF WAR,
captured and taken
far, far, far, far away
from where I iriginate:
AFRIKA,
to work and buil,
work and build,
work and build,

and forced to create
your brutal
vicious
unfair state.
For I
I planned and executed
I escape
dats why I can state

I am not your stereotype
I don't believe
your hype
dat in March 1807
the BRUTISH opened the gates of heaven and set InI
foreparents free and abolished slayvree
I for one will not be
celebrating DAT bicentenary,
when InI enslavers
still cannot say
dat magic word:
SORRY,
and after 500 years
of subjugation
brutality, raping
killing pillage
and depravity,
THOSE EUROPEAN
NATIONS
still can't utter one word of apology
when everyone can see InI peoples reality
(ah wah dem tek dis ting fa?)
still can't utter one word of apology
when everyone can see InI peoples reality
(ah wah dem tek dis ting fa?)

I will not be writing eulogies for Wilberforce
or Granville Sharpe,
who you claim forced you to have a change of heart
but instead I will utter righteous phrases and chant praises
for ones like

Haile Selassie I
Marcus Garvey
Paul Bogle
George William Gordon
Grani Nanny
Sam Sharpe
Tacko
Boukman
Touissant L'Ouverture
Dessalines, Christophe
Harriet Tubman
Queen Nzinga
Yaa Asantewaa
Ya Kimpa Vita
Kwame Nkrumah
Amilcar Cabral
Malcolm X
Zumbi
Martin Luther King Junior , Nelson Mandela
and the countless nameless millions whose names never made it
HISTORY
OURSTORY

CELEBRATE WHA!!!

Gun krayzee

Blak man a
kill Blak man
a kill Blak ooman
a kill Blak man
an I man doan
ovastan
Blak man a
kill Blak man
a kill Blak ooman
a kill Blak man
an I man doan
ovastan

madness
madness
insanitee
iz wa appn
tu ewmanitee
dis kill-a-man
mentalitee
iz aal I man si
dayly, yu si

di gun gun
di gun gun gun gun
di gun gun
di gun gun gun gun
di gun gun
di gun gun gun gun
di gun gun
di gun gun

gun krayzee
dem gaan
gun krayzee
gun krayzee
dem gaan

gun krayzee
gun krayzee
dem gaan
gun krayzee
gun krayzee
dem gaan
gun krayzee

dema watch
tu much
soap opra
play an movie
like bwaiz in di ood
an menis tu soseyeity
dema gwaan like
dema a john wayne
or audi murphy
dem a shape leka
al capone an lewi
lepki
masop claudie
or even rhygin bunny
dats why gunshot
it a bus up
ina evri kontree
ina evri town an vilidge
ina evri sitee
yu wi fine a gunman
ina evri komewnitee
gunshot jus a bus wid nuff regewlaritee
it a kaaz nuff kazhwaltee
n nuff faytalitee
a gunman iz a man wid
no mersee
im wi let arf gunshot
widout pahshlitee
im wi kill di big man
alsu di likkle baybee
im wi separate a man soul from im badee
an lef it

fi a nex man fi kom an beree
im main ambishan
iz fi sen sumwan
tu di semetree
it nu mata if yu inasent
ar if yu giltee
yu tink se a gunman
im a gu sarree
dema yuuz
gun fi mug peepul
an komit rabree
an dema kyaree
shotgun
wen dema bus
ina peepul prapatee
an if aman trya ting dem nuh
fraid
fi yuuz i
dema let aaf
gunshot ina
dancehall
an ina blues partee
NO!!!
I man naa bews up
no gunman posse
kaa dem wi let aaf
gunshot indiskriminetlee
an kill yu an mi an ee an shee
an dem doan giv a dyam whoever it may be
yu si

di gun…

now nuff bullits
ben a fly
between irak an iran
not tu menshan di fitin
dung ina Lebanon
but yu nu si wot a gwaan
na jumayka kingston

dem a kill arf di singaz
an di mewzishans
kaa dem shoot
mayja worries
jammy's mikeman
an dem kill king tubbys
di dub teknishan
an dem kill pan ead
an di wan dertsman
an dem kill peter tosh
yes di mistik man
iz a lang time now
gun feeva
deh pon di eyelan
prince fari woz shot
by a group ov gunman
an hugh mundell woz
a victim ova gunman gang
enuf about jahmayka
wot about inglan
dung a ungafud
di bwai michael ryan
kill sixteen in a orgy
ov distruckshandis gunman bizniz
it a get outta han
chu..

di gun gun............

gunshot ere
gunshot dere
gunshot evriwair
di gunman dem nowadaze
Rasta no dem gaan kleer
di peepul dem ketch
dem fraid an dem
livin in fear
who wants tu live
ina gunman atmosfear
a gunman nu reezn

a gunman nu argyu
i di simplis likle ting
dem wi put a
bullit ina yu
I man nu no iz why
dem a gwaan su
a let arf gunshot
leka dem a Rambo
it mus be de times
dat wi livin in
a sen dem paro
wi afi bruk dung
dis gunman mentalitee
koz truu dis gunman
runnins
nuff wans a get beree
ina gunman runnins
I kuda neva urree
or pon Jah blessed lan
I kuda neva tarree
mi sarree

di gun gun.......

Kokumo

Gerald Dixon, aka Kokumo, was born in Jamaica. He is a Rastafarian. He has lived in Birmingham for many years and is well-known as a dub poet, workshop facilitator and storyteller. For a few years he ran a 'griottology' workshop at the Drum, in Aston, where he has compered several events like the tribute to Louise Bennett in September 2006.

Kokumo visits Jamaica regularly and has worked with the noted dub poet Yasus Afari, releasing a CD single with him entitled *Set it Off*. In 2006 Kokumo released a CD entitled *Writing's on the Wall*, recorded in Birmingham with local musicians. Two interviews with Kokumo can be found on the BBC Birmingham website.

De Machines Keep Rising

Mi si dung an a observe
How de youth dem a guan.
Instead a girl, a gun dem want ina dem arm.
Education out deh, but dem nuh whau learn.
Not even a honest living, dem whau fi earn.
Now the frustration a set een,
Man caan fulfil him dream.
Soh him decide fi rise him steel,
Jus' fi drive a mean machine,
Running de place like a western pon de big screen,
No mercy fi de baby wha a scream.
A humble home become a crime scene.
Wha a cause de senseless killings ?
Whose tasks dem fulfilling ?
To do de devil's work dem willing.
Can't yuh hear Selassie Highs' calling ?
Heed de warning,
Tek a check a yuh life.
Before yuh hit de road dis mauning,
Life is more dan jus' a bad man ting.
Whose war yuh fighting?
An' who is gonna win
Wen yuh destroy all de blakk skin ?
Wi kno' de system set a way
But what do you have to say
Wen yuh destroy de foundation de elders lay
Wen ur existence is in decay ?
Yet everyday yuh hit replay, the same scenario,
Saying it's a jungle out there
An' ur only care is to survive
An' by any means vital
As long as de result is fatal,
Wid de death toll increasing ,
As de machines keep rising
An' de ghetto remain a product a de system
An' its people de likely victims.

In Too Deep

Blinded to the streets,
The codes he never knew.
Not knowing which road to take
Or where to go,
Thinking that everyone he sees
Was a smiling face
Moving in a haste, no hesitate.
So he didn't notice that grin was a fake.
Now his eyes wide open,
He's wide-awake.
Just to realize it's a bit too late
Rise up, wise up
But he was tempted to touch
Not knowing that the first woulda hurt so much.
Now his head is cracked up.
His life is a mess
And the people he trusted is nowhere in sight.
Son, you better check yourself if your doing is right
You know the elders use to have a lot to say.
They said 'listen up';
You didn't care anyway.
They use to say son before you be a man,
There's a few things in life you got to understand.
Knowing who is your enemy
And who to call friend.
Now he's hooked to the streets,
On a leash by the beast.
Abandon his family
Hooked up with so - called friends
Junkies, crackheads
Labeled a failure to society.
Check the reality:
This thing is blowing your mind.
Yet you shacked up in a crack city,
Living in a tower block,
Taking a spiraling flight
Getting high and falling asleep on steep stairways

With prostitutes taking elevated rides,
Up to the twenty seventh floor on their backside.
Millennium junkies, walking around like zombies
Searching for the white lady
To dance for them just one more time.
Hello brotha,
That aint gonna free yah
It's blowing your mind.
Now he's out in the cold,
Didn't consume what's being told
Caressing the cold concrete,
Roaming the street nights after nights.
But the pleasure he seeks
Got him in too deep
Too deep, too deep, too deep
Beep, beep, beep, beep, beep, beep,
Beeeeeeeeeeeeeeeeeeeeeeeep !
Flat line.

Check-Out Mista Govament Man

So the view is beautiful as you sit and twirl
In your skyscrapers,
Remain captivated by the beauty
Of neon lights that shines bright in the city.
But step out and step into my world;
Step out of your first world fantasy and into a third world reality.
Come with me, to the so called ghettos of the world,
Where raw sewage flows underneath your feet.
Come and listen to the belly of a Soweto child speak.
Bare footed children caressing cold concrete in Rio
Dodging ricochet bullets in Kingston's ghetto,
Whilst scavenging for food in a shanty town.
That's the harsh reality, black communities becoming crack city
But not to worry,
Because you can sit in front of your plasma screen
And show pity for starving children in Afrika,
With wind puffed up in their bellies,
While your belly is filled
With the food that had being taken out of their mouth.
The money you donated to charity
To save the children's fun, cannot be found
Because it never got pass administration cost;
And you wonder why there is still starvation
In the countries you stripped of their resources.
The day you take your hands out of our pockets,
And dip it in the ones sitting in your govament office.
The false prophets collecting profits
The so called terrorists won't be suicidal anymore
But be the delivery man at your front door
o before you answer that doorbell,
Thinking the revalushan had being quelled by riot police.
There's a boy from Sierra Leone, holding a AK47 rifle
With one amputated arm.
He lost to the blood diamond on your wife's finger.
There's a child from Iraq who watched his sisters' brain splattered,
His whole life shattered,
A girl from Sudan who can't understand why

She had been raped and her entire family murdered by malitia.
There's a child from Kosovo, with both legs amputated
Trying hard to think how to face the man with the guilt
Because papa had just gotten paid
From dealing in the arms trade
There's a child from Southern Afrika
Questioning why most of her friends are victims of AIDS
So you think it's strange, when I say
None of us are innocent
When we're all forced to pay taxes
To bring your boys home in boxes.
And the truth is, they don't know the real enemies.
Your enemies are not kids throwing stones at tanks
In the West Bank.
Check out the man running the World Bank
Check out mista govament man
Check out the G8 gang.
But now the mute got his speech back,
And the youths' knowledge increasing.
The rebel is about to take your seat.
So the view ain't that beautiful anymore,
When you are about to be dropped
From the top floor
Of the Ebony Tower.
Check out the view
Bus out, Bus out
Mista Govament Man

Storytelling

Sue Brown

Sue Brown was born in Birmingham in 1961. As a performance poet she has worked with musicians and dancers, taking part in various spoken word productions nationally and internationally. She is also a member of 'Writers Without Borders'. Sue Brown has worked in schools, colleges and with many community groups, exploring self-expression, cultural identity and social behaviour. She has also worked as a lecturer at the African Studies Department of the University of Birmingham.

Some of her poems appeared in *Saving the Seeds* (Writers Without Borders, 2006), *Five Birmingham Poets* (Raka Books, 2006), *Bluebeard's Wives* (Heaventree Press, 2007) and *Growing up on Love* (Feather Books, 2008).

Birmingham

Birmingham – this settlement has always been a city of many trades,
Industry, manufacturing and engineering.
In the heart of the country, the revolution made its mark.
With the canals system flowing with rich and varied cargoes,
Commerce was destined to flourish profitably.

From dawn to twinned city
From Beorma to Birmingham
From the outskirts to the Inner Circle
From Bournville to The Bullring
This has always been a city of great diligence
From auction blocks to the first bank
From historical canals to Spaghetti Junction
From small arms manufacturing to the Thinktank
From The Museum & Art Galleries to Chinatown
This has always been a city of great and major influence
From Joseph Sturge to Jamaica
From the MAC to the riots
From Pirate Radio stations to Marcus Garvey Day
From enthused settlers to Poet Laureate
This has always been a city of great demonstration
From Lee Bank to Attwood Green
From the Grand Junction Railways to Fircroft College
From The Lunar Society to Birmingham University
From musical innovators to The Harriett Tubman Bookshop
This has always been a city of great progress
From Bingley Hall to the ICC
From The Cave to The Drum
From woodland clearing to urban villages
From Back-to-Backs to Leisure and Tourism
This has always been a city of great change
From Soho House to Symphony Hall
From Edgbaston Cricket Ground to Carnival
From The River Rea to SeaWorld
From The Town Hall to Spring Hill Library
This has always been a city of great admiration
From Aston Villa to the International Book Festival

From the Shubeens to Broad Street
From the Balti Triangle to the Birmingham Royal Ballet
From the Evening Mail to visiting Heads of State
This has always been a city of great success
From Mathew Boulton to Jasmine Johnson
From John Cadbury to Willard Wigan
From Olaudah Equiano to Benjamin Zephaniah
From Oscar Deutsch to Vanley Burke
This has been a city of great and creative minds
From Herbert Austin to the Jewellery Quarters
From the Rotunda to the Peace Pagoda
From the Botanical Gardens to the Mailbox
From master builder masons to the naturally gifted
This has always been a city of great involvement
From British Nationals to refugees
From yesterdays generation to tomorrows people
From history makers to story tellers
From a city of many cultures to a Star City
This has always been a city of great heritage.

Pain

The pain that **you** brought to my **life** was **like** nothing I had ever experienced
You - penetrated me with such gruelling harshness... alas simulating a
a dirty

              rusty

                          screw trained precisely... into my
soft, warm, tender flesh.
Each jab
         each twist you delivered **razor sharp**
                 pierced my spirit as if searching -
reaching for my soul

The pain that you brought to my life
rendered my senses inoperative - off balance for the longest while
till my ears begun ringing
Each pause you made to catch your breath, only prolong my anguish, my agony, because I knew you'd return with renewed strength and vigour
Excruciating almost to the point of knocking me out you delivered your punches with such sharp accuracy my face became a pillow of heightened sensitivity.
The pain that you brought to my life
Sent me on a journey of self discovery looking for my **recovery**
This meant I had to make a stand and deal with this given situation!
And I did!

The answer was so simple

Today I thank my *dentist* for helping me

Now happily I look back in contentment and of course peace.

It seemed that at one point toothache had the better of me!

From my Thoughts came the Word!

If you were a word
Then I would think of you
Run you through my mind
I would visualise you
Bringing you to sound I would voice you
Shouting you out loudly
I would hear you
Saying you with purpose
I would direct you
If you were a word

If you were a word
Then I would describe you
Finding your root meaning
I would know all about you
Wrapping my tongue around your
Syllables I would pronounce you
Writing you on paper
I would document you
If you were a word

If you were a word
Then I would learn from you
Join you together with other words
I would sentence you
Sometimes compounding
Evening contracting you
Into a paragraph
I would compose you
If you were a word

If you were a word
Then I would express you
Discover your character
I would depict you
Through an etymology
I would know more about you

Using a dictionary
I would understand you
If you were a word
If you were a word
Then I would introduce you
To another language and accent you
Develop you to converse with you
I would gain from you
Sending messages around the world
I would communicate through you
If you were a word.

Michelle Hubbard

Michelle Hubbard, aka The Mother, lives in Nottingham. She has won prizes in many poetry competitions, including Kasa-kasa International Poetry Competition, Seconds Out! Apples 'n' Snakes Manchester Poetry Slam, the Farrago London Poetry Easter Slam + Champions Championship Slam, Nottingham Poetry Society Performance Competition and the Farrago/BBC Radio 4 Slam.

Her books include *The Tapestry of a Black Woman* and *The Irish-Jamaican*. She has also been featured in *Poets In The Pink, Rasta In The Millennium,* and *Ten Years of The Chase*.

Blood lines

My Arabic tongue
Knits Swahili melody
Around my Ethiopian memory

My Caribbean taste buds
Sample a trickle of my Celtic past
As my Eastern Asian eyes
Catch liquid diamonds
From my Native American dreams

Twelfth CD-Track Nine

after Auden

Stop all the computers, switch off the mobile
Keep ya kids from playing with toys for a while
Pause the MP3 but still gently hum
Bring out the coffin, let the morning come

Let the helicopters circle radioing overhead
Texting on their screens the message SORRY MATE HE'S DEAD
Put the CLOSED sign up outside the local pubs
Let the loyal homeboys wear black hoods

He was my blood, my mate, my boy and friend
My chilled out week and my wild weekend
My lyrics, my tunes, my vibes, my ride
He said our fun would last forever. He lied

The CDs are not wanted now: sell them, the lot
Lock away his motorbike. It's over. Forgot
Pour away his dreams then rewind every track
For nothing now can ever bring him back.

Anansi the Spider

This is a story
About Anansi the spider
He gets most everywhere
I wonder if
You've seen him there?

Incey-Wincey spider
Climbed up the spout
NO! - It was Anansi again
Without a doubt!

Little Miss Muffet
Sat on a tuffet
Eating her curds and whey
Along came a spider
Which sat down beside her...
Anansi again I say!

One, two, three, four
Five, six, seven, eight
Legs on a spider...
More Anansi – THAT'S GREAT!!!

He came from Africa
Then went to Jamaica
He went over to America
And even up to Canada

I've studied the evidence
It's all becoming clear
Anansi the spider
Has even been here!

Isn't it great. Isn't it grand
Anansi the spider
Right here in *Eng-a-land!*

Take the Girl out of Notts, but You Can't Take Notts Out of the Girl!

I'm of Nottingham, camouflaged in Robin Hood Green
Making my way through the mighty Sherwood Forest
Loving the smell of fresh pine needles
Bow becomes paper, arrow becomes pen

I am known as The Mother
Jamaican girl with Irish eyes
I am the urban Maid Marion waiting for a surprise
Avoiding the sheriff and his axe
I can't afford my council tax

My house could never be Nottingham's castle
But I sit, happy, on my throne, without hassle
Night clubs full of merry men
That become CCTV legends

Nottingham flows through my veins
Like water down the murky River Trent
Where fish are poisoned alongside the minds of school children
Saturated by stories of that brave *hoody* 'Robin of Nottingham'

Can you see what I see?

In Nottingham we're shotting 'em every day
Boys with toys that blow others away
I see bright youths with so much promise in their eyes
Grope for hope between young girls thighs

I see girls, prettier than *miss world* sold to thugs
I see lost sheep chasing the shepherd for drugs
I see rats following the pied-piper like fools
I see packs, clones, gangs, not proud individuals

I see another teenage brother released on tag
I hear the zzzzzzzip of yet another body bag
I see nine-nights held in local bars
I see a continuous conveyor belt of funeral cars

I see single mothers with broken hearts
I see a crack pipe choke another family apart
I see a desperate mum rob the local shop
Coz dad's Job Seekers Allowance suddenly got stopped

I see young Stacey ain't be feeling too well lately
Unexpectedly she gave birth to a baby
I see overcrowded mental institutions and prisons
I see people walk free for crimes that shouldn't be forgiven

I see so many things that I ain't supposed to see
(And I see it all right here, in Robin Hood Country).

Introspective

Marcia Calame

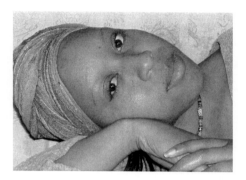

Marcia Calame is a West Midlands-based writer of Caribbean origin. She has been writing poems for many years and has performed at events like Birmingham Artsfest, Black History Month and Glastonbury Festival. Marcia has also read her poems at the Midlands Arts Centre (Birmingham), the Arena Theatre (Wolverhampton), the Glass House (Stourbridge) and the Norden Farm Centre for Arts (Berkshire).

Spring clean

Sometimes my silence hurts me
Especially in my own four walls
As it waits tolerantly outside
My window

Eventually it makes its way
Through the cracks of the frame
It swoops over me like a vampire
To its prey
Swooping towards my neck
Piercing my susceptibility
And draining my quiet
Peace by peace

So, I am then left
With my ears exposed to the
Excessive volumes

The ten times creaking of the stairs
At every step I take
And the fifty times haunting of my thoughts
With every move I make

So, I sweep the brute with my broom
I watch the particles
Loom into the atmosphere
And is carried away in the breeze

The arms of the trees, fan the atmosphere
Like feather dusters
And the zephyr blows a fine mist to freshen the air

Now, there are sounds of children voices
The whistling of the postman
And neighbours banters over the fence

Another mind's Season clear
For another year

Speak English

'Speak English Woman!'
The Queen's English you mean?
Where the 'W' lies steadfast
Emphasised
And heightened in the speech
When I speak?

'She speaks English. Is she British?'

Like a porcelain bread and butter dish
Yorkshire pudding
A slice a beef with lashings of gravy type British?
Perhaps you wish
Me to present my airs and graces

'No need to be angry.'

Then maybe you just think I'm Brutish
I'm not angry
Just hungry

Dis is how mi tark
Fa yu understan' mi wen mi tark like dis

Though nothing English bout my Goat n Rice
Nothing English bout my Rack of Spice
Nothing English bout my bounce when I walk

But dis is how mi wark
Fa yu understan' wen mi wark like dis

English has now become a word of wandering
Perhaps a word of wanting
Maybe needing
Because you understand what you are reading

My character is not part time
A moment in time
Or a pastime
I speak English
A Callaloo and Saltfish type British
Though I may not be the full English
I am real
So here's the deal
Perhaps one day, you and I can sit and together we can eat out
       the same dish

Tree

Like a ghost
She is the silhouette of the woods
Unyielding
Solidly watching your existence
Studying your generation
As you carve the furrowed grooves of your direction
Into her skin
Now this tattoo remains a constant reminder within
Even long after

She has watched you beat yourselves
Before her
And you have scraped your flesh
Against her
Yet still you sit next to her

For comfort
Hugging the barks of her hushed assertion
She senses your tears through her sapwood
Weeping into the earth

To the birth of your beginning
When your little toes and fingers wriggled
In the wind
When your smile blew her leaves gently
Bringing joy directly through her heartwood
And when her leaves fell on your innocent skin
It formed a blanket and warmth within

She is that tree
That sheltered you from all weathers
She is that tree that brought you together
She is that that tree
That nurtured you from the seed
So don't forget me, she said

Many drops of blood
Have spilled around her moss feet
Many heads have rolled along the grass
So many times
She has held on tightly to the fruits
So they can swing carefree
Until the stalks became weak
And are hacked away from her

So be careful how you cut her bark
It is her armour to protect her from transgression

The annual ring of her eyes shows no mercy
Because she has seen so many things that hardens her inner core
And every season, her cambium is an added layer of her soul
But it is her hardwood that will prevent her from breaking
Her sanity

Take a look at her anchor roots
Embedded down below,
Forever creeping around
The fragile bones of yesterday

One day she will hear your outcry
'Timber!'
The echo ness
Will tremor
But she is steadfast

From the seed of the grain
The falling of the rains
Her Son's raise
She will grow again

When her leaves fall from her crown
Like dead hair
Her roots will be done
But not for long
The sun will condition it
And the blue skies will tint it
And her spirit will be again at one

Then it will be combed by the fingers of the new seasons
And it will bloom
Into a lush green Afro

My Mother Roots
My Mother Nature
My Mother forever listening
In the stillness

Camouflage

I am the flower
you have just trod on
I am the wall
you sprayed graffiti on
I am the tree
you have been swinging on
and my branches
are aching, as you are hanging on

I am the soil beneath you
I am the ground too
I am the shoes
with the holes
at the soles
where the rain
soaks right through

I am the canvas you have just painted on
And the pastel colours
you have been working on
To experiment
the shades to paint the face
Of my
expressions
And my skin
Into
One
I am the mind
channelling
Your thought
Through the brush
To perfect
that artistry

I am the ink
That prints
So you can read me

Take a look closely
Can you
see
me ?

Going Dutch

Give me your pot
and I will teach you Dutch
My Mother's wooden spoon
With the handle broke
just enough seasoning with that heritage touch
Let me teach you Dutch
Let me show you pot

Let's appreciate our pride
Why hide the truth
When you know the truth will surface?
If not through you
Then through our youths

My good sista
Hear me brodda
Nu'un nah go fill you wid just pasta
Microwave cooking and instant soup
The list can go on
wid yu crouton
and en croute
Tell me where your seeds lie
In the land of your soul?

A piece a lettuce here
An' a cucumber there
And not a sight of Callaloo anywhere
No breadfruit
No cornmeal porridge
No stew peas
No proper roughage
To get rid of that contravention
From the bowls of discrimination

Give me your pot
and I will teach you Dutch
My Mother's wooden spoon

With the handle broke
Just enough seasoning with that heritage touch
Let me teach you Dutch
Let me show you pot

Martin Glynn

Martin Glynn was born in Nottingham in 1957. He has been active as a performance poet since the early 1980s and his work has appeared in numerous anthologies. He was one of the poets included in the pioneering anthology edited by the German critic Christian Habekost *Dub Poetry: 19 Poets from England and Jamaica* (Michael Schwinn, 1986).

His collections of poems include *De Ratchet A Talk* (Akira Press, 1985), *Angola* (Curious Press, 1990), *Ancestral Whispers* (Triangle, 1993) and *Griot Excursion* (Shomari Productions, 1995).

Martin has gained a national and International reputation for his commissioned work in theatre, radio drama, live literature, and poetry. He has recently completed several full-length screenplays; *The Haunting of Hip-Hop, Broken Fish,* and *Stoneface*. He has also written two novels for reluctant readers, *Bad Brother* (2008) and *Blood Bond* (2008). He is also featured in several poetry anthologies published by McMillan, and recently released his first eBook of poems and short stories, *Shadow People*.

Where It's At

Holding back
Holding it in
Bolted facial expressions
Push it back
Preventing the flow
Cheek muscles twitching.
'Don't let it go',
Your pride whispers.
Deep breathing,
Deeper breathing.
Out the nose... loudly,
Through the mouth... even louder.
Swallowing hard,
Windpipe vibrating.
Pursed lips flickering,
Eyes closing slowly,
Eyes watering,
Heart racing,
Feet pacing.
Becoming helpless,
Losing control.
Lost control.
Feeling embarassed,
Feeling relieved.
I've done it,
I've cried.
THAT'S
WHERE...
IT'S...
AT...

Dizzy

The teacher,
The preacher
Who got down
And
... reached yer.
Told the Scripture,
With rapture,
To capture
The essence
With presence,
Who told it
Like it is;
The sparkle
With the fizz
Kicked the butt,
Be-bop strut,
Cheeks puffed up,
Told with pride,
Couldn't hideThe laughter
Of the story.
Took the glory
We knew,
When he blew,
Always came thru.
REST
IN PEACE,
DIZ.

from To Whom It May Concern

And so the journey begins
Mum came from Walez ... dad from Jamaica
Traced my cultral roots .. Eshu from Nigeria
I woz one of twins ... at birth my brotha died
He neva had a name .. I neva grieved and neva cried
Union of da two ... placed mi in between
Half-caste .. mongrel ...mixed race ... termz made me feel unclean
Curly hair ... light skin ... alwayz bein' put down
Emotionally mixed up ... an old buildin' within a new town

Mum gave birth ter dis innocent child
Anotha brotha from da ghetto ... born gentle 'n' mild
Dad walked out wen I woz one year old
No dogs ... irish ... coloureds ... thatz what wi were told
Dad was a nomad ... so we lived on our own
Struggled with my life .. so I chose to go it alone
Lived in nuff places before da age of five
Mum continued to struggle ... but she kept us all alive

Then she met a Whiteman ... became his house keeper
Racial tauntin' .. an' abuse .. anga jus' got deeper
Black and White alike ... red alert an' then attack
Both sidez sed da same ting .. *'rememba you're half Black'*
At school I blended in well ...
Till da black yout's made a noise an' a din ...
Then I woz seen az black an' outrageous
An' judged by da tone of my skin.
An old blackman said, *'Who is yu mudder?'.*
I replied, *'My mother, she's white'* ...
Hiz stare at that point woz quite vacant
Like a man bein' mugged in da night.
A friend said *'you're so lucky ... bein' two people rolled into one'*
I said *'how can I be lucky? I didn't know what head to put on'.*
West Indies were playin' England ... nuff prestige at stake.
I wanna take a side ...go on ...
Tell me what side should I take?

Then thru' stupidity… I came unstuck
Had a fight wid a bredrin .. now my leg was bruk
Couldn't walk .. pushed me further into fear
Not only felt despondent .. but killed off my career
Alwayz wished I'd had the company of my brotha
Neva talkin' about my loss … not even with my motha

You see
I'm no longer
Bound by notions of race
I'm no longer
Held captive or lost without trace
I'm no longer
Tied to the tone of my skin
I'm no longer
Imprisoned by the darkness within
I'm no longer
Oppressed by biased assumptions
I'm no longer
Driven by greed 'n' consumption
I'm no longer
Smelling the aroma of fear
I'm no longer
Scared of shedding a tear
I'm no longer
Worried 'bout *'Keepin' it real'*
I'm no longer
Bothered by havin' to feel
I'm no longer
Wrapped up in status or ego
I'm no longer
Fearful of lettin' the past go
I'm no longer
Trapped by bein' told I'm not equal
I'm no longer
Concerned with reruns or sequels
I'm no longer
Frightened to talk from the heart

I'm no longer
Annoyed at going back to the start
I'm no longer
Engaged in keepin' myself down
I'm no longer
Hateful of those who want me to drown
I'm no longer
Concealing or hiding the truth
I'm no longer
In denial coz I'm living proof
That freedom
Ain't a mystery
Nor wrapped up in clues
Or based on a theory
Or a line in the blues
Or made out of wood
Or grown from the soil
Or shaped out of mud
Freedom is right now
I just have to take it

Roy McFarlane

Roy McFarlane was born in Birmingham of Jamaican parentage. He is a Community Development Worker for Dudley and Walsall Mental Health Trust. His play *For the Love of Auset* was premiered at The Drum, Aston, in 2007. He is a former Starbucks poet in residence and a member of the New October Poets. He is currently Birmingham's Poet Laureate.

A Black Man in Wolverhampton

I've always wondered why Black people
Came to Wolverhampton,
That place just off the M6
In the middle of nowhere.

Queen Victoria called it the Black Country,
Black Country! Black people!
Where else would we go?

It's the place of the 'Yam, Yam'.
Well Black people nyam yam,
Sweet potatoes and tings.

Yow spake funny, 'yam bostin'.
We felt at home with people
Who couldn't speak the Queen's English.

The black and gold of the Wolves
And myths of streets paved with gold
Only to find Blacks and Irish on Waterloo Road.

Migration is nothing new, just ask the Manders
Those bloody foreigners
Who moved across the Welsh border.

So why did Enoch speak of forebode?
River Tiber foaming with much blood
When racism had already spilt our blood

And look at the bronze Lady Wulfruna
Like the statue of liberty
Welcoming the poor and the needy

Instead they were welcomed with closed doors,
Cold looks and biting words
In a bitter climate.

I've always wondered why Black people
Came to Wolverhampton
That place just off the M6
In the middle of nowhere.

Out of the darkness cometh light

It's snowing outside

It's snowing outside,
Well I was glad it wasn't snowing inside
With all the commotions,
People mixed with emotions,
And faces fixated with nature's splendour.

It wasn't as if we're at the equator's line
Or basking in blazing sunshine.
A November night in middle England,
Somebody please make me understand
When people say it's snowing outside.

It's snowing outside, yeah! I know,
You'd think it was Hailey's comet on show,
Maybe because it's too warm to snow,
And how can it be too cold to snow,
It's bloody England it's bound to snow.

I suppose that's what brings a whole country
To a standstill, apparently
Two inches of snow and total disorder
With gritters waiting for an order
Saying it's snowing outside.

The only time we ever prepare,
Is a time when snow never seems to appear
Waiting with great expectations on Christmas Day.
And I'm sure you'll catch a bookie pray,
'Please God I hope it's not snowing outside.'

Playing Jazz

This is the closest
I'll ever get to playing Jazz
A double bass voice
Pulling strings of poetry
Singing melodies of Jazzoetry

This is my A-train to Dixieland
Doing ragtime and big band
My strange fruit hanging from the poplar tree
Telling our struggles and our liberty
Finding God in a Love Supreme,
A Love Supreme, A Love Supreme,

And Round about midnight I'm in a day dream
Flying like Bird to the top
Doing be-bop, hard-bop till I can't stop
Making me feel kind of blue
Caught up in a Witches brew

This is the closest
I'll ever get to playing Jazz
A double bass voice
Pulling strings of poetry
Singing melodies of Jazzoetry

Leaving me in throes of ecstasy

The first time I met poetry
She grabbed ahold of me
And left me in throes of ecstasy
Then when she was finished
She whispered softly and tenderly
That this was my destiny

I've seen her in all her beautiful colours
As Nubian as the night
And bright as the morning light

I've seen rooms filled with gloom
That when she walks in
The dead rise from the tomb

I've seen people so engrossed
That they're no longer overdosed
And comatose with the cares of this life

I've seen her draw so near
That hidden fears
Escape in tears

I've seen her baptize
Watch demons exorcized
Leaving spirits harmonised

You see, like Tinkerbelle
She's already woven her spell
Leaving me all compelled

Like a moth drawn to the fire
Caught up in her desire
I become a living pyre

The first time I met poetry
She grabbed ahold of me

And left me in throes of ecstasy
That when she was finished
She whispered softly and tenderly
That this was my destiny.

I found my father's love letters

I found my father's love letters
in strange and obscure places
often hidden in dark secret spaces,
where memories had closed the doors.

I found blank letters, with matching cards and envelopes.
A small draw filled with letters unfinished,
crossed through, curling at the edges,
turning in the colour of time.

There was one in Marquez's *Love in a time of Cholera*
sandwiched somewhere between
Fermina's rejection of Floretina
and a lifetime of loving, waiting for true love.

I found some penned in a note pad, half-written, half-thought,
scribbled to capture fleeting thoughts,
earnest in writing the emotional overflow
that time edits into streams flowing over with love.

I found one folded
lost in the attic
an elegy to love
that time had forgotten.

I searched to find the true name to those letters entitled *my love*.
A secret lover? Distant lover? First time lover?
or even my mother of whom you gave a thousand names
but I never heard you call her *my love*.

I wonder if they ever received their letters,
an amended version, a completed version
refined and acceptable, filled with rose petals,
signed and sealed with your love.

Chester Morrison

Chester Morrrison is a poet and storyteller and is a member of Black Readers and Writers. He has performed his poetry widely with Jean 'Binta' Breeze and others, won poetry slams and read his poems at youth centres, schools and community centres. He recently performed his *Untold Stories: Tribute to Curtis Mayfield and Buju Bantu* at City Voices in Wolverhampton.

Can You Hear

Do you write for blacks? He asked
I write for Black people, I said
Do you write for all kinds of blacks?
People. Yes I said, working class
Middle class and upper class
Black people
Upper class blacks! He exclaimed
People. I said
His face distorted
As he gave birth
To another thought
Do you write for us? He asked
White people? Yes, I said
Working class, middle class
and upper class white people
Oh. He said.
His knitted brow
And quivering lips
Signalled the emergence
Of another thought
Yes, I said
For any one who cares
Listens, reads, hears
Or dares to understand.

Reading

Reading is something, we should all enjoy
Whether we are men, women, girls or boys
It opens the world, so that we can see
Dimensions of life, or how it could be

Reading helps, to build imagination
Raise understanding, of our situation
It takes us to places near and far
And we don't need to be, a famous star

Reading is not, the preserve of a few
It's open to people, like me and you
And even if it gets, ubiquitous
Everybody knows, it remains precious

Reading aids, connections to the past
Reminds us of the schemes, which did not last
It unveils the picture, it tells a story
Though not everyone is seen, in full glory

Recently I had, something on my mine
I spoke to a friend, who never had the time
So I read a book, to try work it out
Before my friend returned it cleared my doubts

Now my book sits proudly, upon its shelf
Anytime I want, I can help myself
It keeps my secrets and it don't forget
The most reliable friend, I've found yet.

Some Black Men

There are Black men on the ground
there are Black men in the air
yet Black women are saying
they can't find them in their sphere.

Black men a succeed
and Black men a fail
though most of dem free
Some a languished in jail.

Black men in a work
Black men looking for a job
Some a dem a prosper
Some a dem a get rob.

Black men in a marriage
some a dem single
Black men a recluse
Some just love to mingle

Some Black men have tried
And some are trying
Some Black men need love
Not your despising.

Some Black men a lion
Some Black men a mouse
Some a dem homeless
Some have fancy house

Some Black men are short
Some Black men are tall
Some Black men are slim
Some round like a ball.

Some Black men a dunce
Some in education
Some live life for fun
Some a build dem nation.

Some Black men are handsome
Some are very ugly
Some dem children don't know
Some love dem family.

Some Black men are fools
Some Black men are wise
Some hate de limelight
Some love to advertise.

Some Black men are shaky
Some solid like rock
Some dip in dip out
Some never look back.

Some Black men are quiet
Some are garrulous
Some love anybody
Some love only us.

Some Black men can do
What some Black men can't
Tell me now sisters
Is which Black man you want?

Slam

Dreadlockalien

Richard Grant, aka Dreadlockalien, is well-known as a performance poet, workshop facilitator and slam champion. A chef by trade, he started writing poetry after reading Benjamin Zephaniah's *City Psalms* while at university. In 2003 he won the National Slam Championship in Oxford, and in 2005-2006 he was Birmingham Poet Laureate. He founded the New October Poets collective with Kokumo and Moqapi Selassie, later the Colour Free Visions Team, an organisation which takes poetry to schools and uses oral poetry like slam and grime to reduce illiteracy rates. Because he is wholly committed to the oral tradition, his poetry has rarely appeared in print before.

White as a Ghost

White as a ghost, indicating a sheet pale skinned reaction of fear.
Black sheep, ba ba family outcast, sore thumb not welcome here
White lightning, striking bolts, connect charged protons gathering pace
Black thunder, deep rumble, grumble of the god's, and booming bass.
White water rapids giving white knuckle rides.
Blackberry, fruits nestled amongst thorns on roadsides
White lie is still a lie but because it's white then its okay
Blackmail is extortion over something that I might as a man may say.
Whiteboard political correctness replaces chalk and dust
Black spot is a place where accidents often take place, a corner we don't trust
Blackjack is twenty one or bust
Black flag, stop the race. It's all over.
White cliffs now we all know that's the sight of dover
Black ice carpets skating cars, gliding sideways to barriers, chaos and disorder
Whitefriars, not English chippies but monks of a preordained order.
Blackamoor sculptures of subservience, leafed in golden opulence
White elephants, a rare concept that seems to defy common sense
Black out, well I was going anyway,
Whitewash blankets everything that I have to say
Blackburn was once a verb not a place name
White feathers are sent to those who do not play the game
Blackbirds, rooks, ravens, john crows all look the same
What's in a colour, what's in a name ?
What's in a colour, what's in a name?

I am whatever colour you see...

I am that scorched look you sit out in summer for
I am dark stained Pine, antique cupboard door
I am shaded latino who's on the dance floor
I am the colour of the exotic other,
I am olive from dad and ebony from my mother
I am Chocolate, dark, milk and white
I am the Bronze that flashes throughout the night
I am the colour of rain soaked Rust
I am the beige bloke you don't like to trust
I am that Oak coloured chestnut roasted on open fires
I am that tub of fake sun tan that your ego so desire
I am that caramel bar, melting in the heat
I am that burnt toffee cinder, sugar clad and sweet
I am tarnished copper, I am unpolished brass
I am the sandlewood sojourner that you just walk past
I am the dark that's between the handsome and tall
I am that subtle shade of sandstone wall
I am that coloured sense of an Autumn sunrise
I am that dark umber that many still despise
I am the colour of 6 billion eyes.
I am the grey of the middle ground starting to rise
I am that single drop of cream in your Columbian coffee cup
I am tan, I am sable, I am cinnamon, I am a hint of roasted nut
I am the colour of freshly dug mother earth
I am mulatto, mixed up from birth
I am Cherokee, mahogany, a darker shade of pale,
I am Nubian, autumn blossom, The colour of real ale.
I am mocha, terracotta, mustard seed & Teak,
I am the tone of Raw Sienna, totally unique
I am that golden glint that glistens on your chain
I got a eumelanin overload running through my brain
I am that toasted shade of hot almond flakes.
I am that cocoa powder you shake over cakes
I am a palette mix of magnolia and wood smoke
To me colours are just not a joke.
So when you give me a tick box please get it right.
If colour is what you see then who is black or white?

I'm an Anglo Indo Caribbean

I'm an an Anglo Indo Caribbean
As soh me ansa dem who seh 'A whe u cam fram?'
Let me tell U lickle story
Call it history lesson.
A me dem come fi tell you bout indentured Indian.

Uno all hear of slavery an its abolition
Well a who den plant u sugar ?
a de One Indian

Me great great grandma Solanta Bika was her name
Tricked from her homeland
Never to see again
Passage from India, exchanged at Liverpool docks.
Paraded like a catwalk queen
hen locked back up a stocks
Stocks….stock…..

A she did breed we coolie stock
Me Granpa mek money pan butchers block
Send me puppa to go to school prove he was no yardie fool
Come to Henglan   tt   tt   tt   1964   tt   tt   tt
Not long before they closed the door.
Flew over on an apprenticeship
Pack up im clothes an him pack up is grip
Yeah you know u going on a one way trip
Put up u foot man u deserve i

Second generation now is revealing
Blackness… all of a sudden is culturally appealing
As my children get lighter an lighter
My future looks whiter an whiter!
Me bawl.. A few drops of colour innah white paint pot

Stir for a decade you will see it not.
The policy of labour migration
Followed by a process of assimilation

Ask yourself the question
Will this really lead to a multi-coloured nation ?
Or simply the birth of a less dark English creation.?

Evoke

Born in Birmingham, Shaun Welch, aka Evoke, grew up in the Walsall area. Evoke is a young rap/grime/spoken word artist and a new addition to the West Midlands performance poetry scene.

He already has a formidable reputation as a spoken-word artist and over the last few years has appeared at various festivals, and at many 'open mic' sessions throughout the West Midlands. He has also worked as a workshop facilitator in schools.

The Inner You

By looking at the world,
We can see what's within us.
To get to know the inner you,
You have to watch the things you do.
Everything you say,
Everything you do,
Everything you create,
Is an expression of who you are...Inside.
You say the world is full of hate and beauty,
Anger and pleasures,
Mistrust and beliefs,
Lust and hope,
Violence and love,
War and family,
Pain and peace,
Oppression and life,
Death and laughter,
Depression and fun,
Tears and smiles,
Poverty and youth,
Politics and memories,
Secrets and stories,
Deceit and light,
Darkness and truth,
Yet, you fail to see that all this is just a representation of...
You.

We

We no longer look for happiness because we're constantly seeking results…
We want to get there quick and easy we said…
We want to know how without looking…
We're not too fussed about the, whom unless they got the, what…
And sharing time is something we don't deal in often
Because we spend most of it asking when…
When will we get ours?
Who will we get it off?
What will we get?
Where will we get it from?
Why haven't we got it yet?
Maybe because 'you' rarely act as 'we'
And only think about the, 'me' you said…
We may never find the happiness, if 'we' keep seeking 'me' results.
You said.

Further Reading

James Berry (ed) *Bluefoot Traveller* (Harrap, 1976)

James Berry, *News for Babylon* (Chatto and Windus, 1984)

David Dabybeen and Nana Wilson-Tagoe, *A Reader's Guide to West Indian and Black British Literature* (Hansib, 1988)

Bernadine Evaristo and Daljit Nagra (eds) *Ten New Poets Spread the Word* (Bloodaxe, Northumberland, 2010)

Kwame Dawes and Kadija Sesay (eds) *Red:Contemporary Black British Poetry* (Peepal Tree Press, Leeds, 2010)

Prabhu Guptara (ed) *Black British Literature: An Annotated Bibliography* (Dangaroo Press, 1986)

Christian Habekost (ed) *Dub Poetry:19 Poets from England and Jamaica* (Michael Scwinn, Neuestadt, 1986)

Asher and Martin Hoyles, *Moving Voices: Black Performance Poetry* (Hansib, 2002)

Kwesi, Owusu (ed) *Black British Culture and Society. A Text Reader*. London: Routledge, 2000.

Sesay, Kadija, ed. *Burning Words, Flaming Images. Poems and Short Stories by Writers of African Descent* (S.A.K.S Publications, 1996)

Kadija Sesay and Courttia Newland (eds) *IC3 –The Penguin Book of New Black Writing in Britain* (Penguin, 2000)

Kadija. Sesay, *Write Black, Write British; from Post Colonial to Black British Literature* (Hansib, 2005)

Lemm, Sissay (ed) *The Fire People: A Collection of Contemporary Black British Poets* (Payback Press, Edinburgh, 1998)

Onyekachi, Wambu (ed) *Empire Windrush. Fifty Years of Writing about Black Britain* (Victor Gollancz, 1998)